ARIOSO

Selected Poems

ARIOSO

Selected Poems

Carol Adler

A Dandelion Books Publication
www.dandelion-books.com

Dandelion Books, LLC
Mesa, Arizona

Adler, Carol
Arioso: selected poems – hard copy edition
ISBN 978-1-893302-99-0, 1-934280-58-5
Library of Congress Control Number 2010934429

Cover Art by Bill Austin@ www.HealingHolograms.com
Book cover and interior design by Accurance @www.accurance.com

ARIOSO was first published in e-book edition in 2008 by Dandelion Books, LLC.

Dandelion Books, LLC
www.dandelion-books.com

In one creative thought a thousand forgotten nights of love revive, filling it with sublimity and exaltation. And those who come together in the night and are entwined in rocking delight do an earnest work and gather sweetnesses, gather depth and strength for the song of some coming poet, who will arise to speak of ecstasies beyond telling.

—Rainer Maria Rilke

All of the poems in this collection were published previously in other works by Carol Adler:

Arioso [Pentagram Press, 1975]
First Reading [Northwoods Press, 1985]
Still Telling [Northwoods Press, 1987]

Over 75 of these poems were also published previously in a number of literary magazines, newspapers and journals.

Other Books by Carol Adler

Non-Fiction

Writers, Authors & Dream Weavers: I Heard Your Call For HELP! How to Write Non-Fiction, Fiction, Poetry, Memoirs, Children's Stories… and More (hard copy & ebook)

How To Publish & Market a Book Without Jumping Off a Cliff (ebook)
http://www.dandelion-books.com/publish-it.html

Do You Really Need To Write A Book? Tips & Techniques For Writing, Publishing, Marketing & Promoting YOUR BOOK! (hard copy & ebook download)
http://www.dandelion-books.com/writes-Carol-Adler.html

Fiction

Come as You Are (by Sarah Daniels, a pseudonym) (hard copy & ebook)

Slouching Past Bethlehem (hard copy and ebook download)
http://www.dandelion-books.com/Dandelion-Downloads.html

The Woman With Qualities (by Sarah Daniels, a pseudonym) (hard copy & ebook)

Poetry

Jesus & The Tooth Fairy – Poems by Carol Adler (ebook)
http://www.dandelion-books.com/Jesus-and-the-tooth-fairy.html

Naked in Daylight (ebook)
http://www.dandelion-books.com/naked-in-daylight.html

Shaelot (Questions) (hard copy & ebook download)
http://www.dandelion-books.com/carol-adler-questions.html

Contents

ARIOSO

arioso   bells
sepia
moon-beams
an afternoon sun blanked by rain
and the mountains rising nowhere
the sound returns
                        the sound and the silence   chimes

STARTING OUT

anywhere is wide enough
as long as you find it
already reserved by
readiness

a leaping clear
to the feel of it
reassurance
that this is you

any space
even God
will do

ETUDE

And are we not after all
pinned to our destiny
to some sense of ourselves
that has been carefully laid out

that will eventually slip over us
with the same surety
as tomorrow's past—

Offered this consciousness
as the only one
and forced to accept it
as something earned or
bargained for
before we were born

and for which
no words
will let us express
exactly what it is to be here
at this moment

and the fact that
we are that
very miracle

in the dawn's first opening

images
must be learned

by rows of eyes
reciting

DAWN

He falls to his knees
burying his head
in her lap

promising her
a gold crown
the moon
anything—

and she believes
learning too late

how naïve she was
how trusting:

that what she is asked
to give in
return

after consenting

is what he has used
for his coins.

Oh she bleeds
she bleeds . . .

OUR AMAZEMENT

our amazement was the dawn to play with
how we pulled and tousled with it
each of us in our separateness   each of us
bound to this beginning
devil to the one we tried to do away with
as we did away with ourselves

what were we afraid of   what ceremony
did we expect to witness
as we stared into the future
refusing this image   yet bound to it as
if to some awareness   was it
Thanatopsis   longing for the Great Deliverer

or was it adolescence
the first defiant kiss

why shouldn't
the lightning take lovers   the hills
stop repeating themselves

ELEMENTAL AIR

Over thirty years ago
when I was a poet
I used to spend my days
contemplating daily occurrences
of Inexplicable Phenomena:

For example
The Setting Sun.

Perched outside
on a slab of pale pink cement
heavily fortified against
mosquitoes and ticks
I would lift my eyes
to the Heavens and rivet them
on the vast Cosmogeny of
Plethoric Sound

Raging Plenaries that could
easily with a Master's touch
my own
be trapped and tamed
until seemingly emerging
from the pores of my Being
as Being Itself
becomes prismic emanations:

glittering jewels of *mot juste*
that would greedily be
gobbled up
published and praised
in leading journals . . .
Chewing on the tip of my pen
I pondered
how to begin.

Similes or metaphors
fables . . . myths . . .
analogies of rivers and streams
references to forgotten dreams . . .

or maybe just with water itself
or elemental air
parts of the body
fingers eyes cheeks hair

gestures intimations
significant conversations

And as I sat there
Shivering   for it was early
June and my soul laid bare
had only a cotton tee shirt
and cutoffs
to cover it

as I sat there Communing
suddenly I felt
somewhere in the vicinity of hunger
a hollowness
and in my head a loosening.

Then I felt myself lifting
and yes now recklessly taking off
soaring at incalculable velocities
West in the direction
of the disappearing sun.

But the faster I traveled
the faster ahead of me
the scene receded

and the more urgently I pushed on
the greater the distance between
what was supposed to be
described and what was
already dying

the tongue the flame
the ruby tip of tingling pain
drowning in confused consummation
of what was already done
before I'd even begun

blank pad growing pink
pink slab growing black
black to white white
to black the blackest night
that any poet has ever
attempted to write about
now
and then

BLUEBERRIES

While God is in His heaven
eating just-picked blueberries

I am in the Adirondacks
with my father
wading through the grass
searching for ripened patches.

Each day before breakfast
the two of us
working the field
until in no time
we're swinging back to the
cabin our brimming buckets
weightless.

I think we could have picked
forever and still
there would be more
as if we were not taking
from the mountains
but giving.

For now even though it's
September
as I set the table for
one and heap my dish with
frozen berries

I see in my mirror
the fields
still full
and the sun
just risen.

FIRST AUTUMN

against
the wind the young
maple bleeds until her
leaves are drenched with
living

AUTUMNAL

the corn is cold
the ground is cold

each depth uncovers
the same tissue

each death evokes
the same calling

HARVEST

this morning
when the words went away

I lost myself
though I kept saying

such lapses
are normal

time gives back
what the mind cannot

so i set my feet in
another direction

and took a walk
where i'd never been

on the way
closing my eyes and

collecting some raindrops
carved by the wind

MARKINGS

It rained last night
and when I went out
before dawn

even though the moon
was gone and the
stars were covered

I found my way
by following
the hollows where the
water had been trapped.

Black on black
they shone as if
with a light of their own.

But when I came to the
spot of the Broken Heart
it was totally dark

with nothing to
follow but a yellow line

and the silvered scars
on the bark of a tree:

Nothing to follow
but a map of pain

that guided me
with certainty.

HERE

There's a place
I keep coming back to

as if I thought I'd left
something behind

or as if my mind
was unable to go anywhere else
without first finding myself
there—

This place
a mountain lake   field of grain
woodsmoke   the morning
sun   a picket fence
swinging gate

or any obstruction
that forces me
to cancel out
everything
but the fact that
this is me
and the place is mine

this passion deep within
cold to consequence
oblivious to pain.

SHORELINE

far out
nothing but more of the same
indiscriminate grayish-white

but close-up
orbiting at our feet
tiny galaxies of grass poking
out of the sand

each pooled by its own
nimbus made by the wind
you said as it twirled them around
forcing them to mark
their own perimeters

far out
nothing
and close up only
the pin-and-chalk
of our marked destinies

plant me in the sand i said
so i can wait for the wind to
show me

then stretch the string
beyond each point

so when you and i
walk the shore
and look out

each day will be a marked
event circled by more
of the same
nothing visible far out
and close-up
only what you and i
choose to be

WIRES TELEPHONIC (SQUIRRELS GAZING)

After Richard Eberhart

Whirling in the cornucopia of the invisible
ear's trumpeting

he was oblivious to his own expertise
so in a sense superior;

and although these wires were meant
neither for humans nor squirrels

it was for each indubitably
the neatest way to cross the street.

Yet if I were he,
Even if licensed—I know I
would not risk it—at least
not without a net.

Nor would I dare the go-between
of any trafficked height

not so much I think for the danger of it
as for the specter
of myself floating above the cement
giving all who chanced to look up
adequate reason for comment.

Then there's always the end—
Who could tell what would happen

once the gossip having finished
and some argument begun: invading
enemy air space, ignorant or ill-advised—
the very sky would seem to hum.

Are those wires strong enough
or would they snap? And what if
some storm grabbing hold of them
chewed them off

leaving me there dangling mid-air—
wide open for pedestrian fare?

Yet to a squirrel
if a squirrel can master parallels

we would probably seem equally ridiculous,
deliberately shooting ourselves off
wireless

or scampering back and forth
between two poles, discovering ourselves

too late ensnarled in the wrong extreme.

So what do squirrels and humans share
but a harlequin faith

meant neither for them nor us
nor for anyone else who might be

slightly Messianic . . .

MELONS PEACHES AND CORN

For the Sweeneys

When winter's moon hangs in the sky
orange and succulent
and over the snow the
ears of early morning light
fill out with yellowing kernels

when the down of sun takes on a
rosy blush

hungrily I stalk the fields
plunging into oceanic craters
ripping off husk and silk
of every orb
gouging into skin and pulp

letting the juice dribble
from my chin
and sweeten the ground
like the freshest dew

until there seems to spring
from hidden sources
golden fruit.

These visions
harvesting from frozen fields
memories of tomorrow's yield.

NIGHT BLIZZARD

At 3 AM
hardly awakened
by the plow:

for it was the silence
of the falling snow
that had alerted us

to the harsh grating

warning us to clear the streets
we tried.

But the streets filled up
too fast

and the snow came
predictably too soon.

Stranded,
should we atone?

For according to the Almanac
we should never have
set out

and according to the
traffic
even from the start
we were doomed.

RIPOSTE: THE COUNTING

Now the hunt is over
and all the stars are shot down.

They lie
in the sun-dark snow

wounded, still,
while the sky goes on

goes on
hopelessly listing . . .

a flake becomes a leaf
and a leaf becomes a flake

a stone a stone

IRONIES

dried-up rivers
that still keep flowing

fields harvested
that keep growing

silence

                    yielding

INSOMNIA

Somewhere the distance
yowls
awakening the night.
It leaps up on the ledge
searching.

There must have been an
accident.
Someone has died
or been murdered.

The clock screeches to a halt
before the mottled body

and the stars collect
one by one
afraid to look.

By the time the
squad car arrives
it's already too late—

all evidence has been cleared
and the victims
devoured.

Daylight comes red-eyed but
innocent
its damp paws licked
clean.

NIGHT SONG

If there should be crying
that nobody hears
or hands that spill empty
eyes that spell fear

then let me be chosen
to fill those hands
and dry those tears.

Let me be appointed
to put up stakes
drop crumbs
or leave something behind

so when night closes in
refusing the dawn
when hope that was given
is already gone

at least I can lend you
from the sigh of the wind
or sweep or a wing
soaring upward

a little grace
a little sign.

SPRING

Painting by Marc Chagall

Spring, you Goat!

What kind of a ferkockney
instrument is a green
Violin

I sit on your shoulder
sucking your ear like an infant

but you go on fiddling
beating me with your bow

till I bleed into bloom

HIGH LOOM WEAVING

First
accepting the given

next glancing up
to perceive
the immediate
just-finished design

then
climbing the ladder
and starting in

blindly
yet with all the passion and
zest of one obsessed
with deliverance

thrusting the shuttle
in and out
pausing only long enough
to acknowledge the distance
and discrepancy

between partial patterns
and finished lines
of what can be learned
that remains unknown

what can be seen
that cannot be shown.

IT IS THE PURE SHAPE

it is the pure shape
the stone prism
water
clarified by wood

the pure shape of meeting
the small separations and the change
the leaving behind and

falling part

the pure shape of pain
a child's wonder
when first discovering the dawn
that makes division permanent

TERROR

terror is a short-live nightmare
until it is real

then there is an equalization

THERE ARE DIFFERENT DEGREES

there are different degrees of
terror

different bits of glass
in the eye's cathedral

TOO LITTLE TO REACH

too little to reach
and tall enough to want
that

is the paradox

BLESSINGS

are the flesh-colored necklaces
with their weightless medallions

invisible sky-pulleys and
electric buttons that monitor
the stars.

And when time stacks itself up
in balanced promises
they are the jokers
who pull out the air

you and me
moving through them
mindlessly
unaware.

YOUR HOUSE

Your house is too large for me
it has too many doors
I can never decide which
I should enter
too many rooms
I can never decide
which should be mine

the ceilings are too high
I get lost looking up
I get lost looking down
and when I go in

I get lost looking out
I get lost looking in
behind my back
the windows add and multiply
and each night when they cancel out
they come back at me
like ghosts
like too many mirrors
with their clouded images
all of them
failing to remember

So I pick up a stick
pretending to threaten them
but they too pick one up
and another and another
and the sticks multiply
making a fence
too high with a
gate locked and

painted over
so again I'm out
when I'm supposed to be in
and again I get lost

I get lost in the garden
someone has given me the
wrong map the wrong
information
and the only stairs I can
find lead down
to the part unfinished
where I keep falling asleep
hoping to get in

and in my sleep I keep
calling out
asking as if anyone's home
but since no one answers
as if someone can
I go in anyway
breaking in like a tramp
or a thief
or a messenger bearing
something else
besides myself
that should somehow matter

room after room
I go in and come out
I go in and come out
the other side
coming through
coming out
wordless
and empty

so I keep asking
I keep asking
like a broken record
or a broken clock
is it really for me
this heart
this nakedness
that you the builder
my body my tongue
keep offering me
again and again
lifting it over me
like a blessing as if
it should fit

UNITED NATIONS

Who stole the steps
so carefully laid out?

Who smashed the armature,
who seized the bar—

this flag
a rag

promises mere threats . . .

Have we erred again,
hammering only these

hollows?

Who can repair
God's despair?

The hunger-war
is the only war

and the enemy-eye only
the one inside.

Feed me
it cries

feed me with lies
about peace.

Peace.

It cries like
a broken
record.

DEFIANCE

I was not meant to bear signs
nor was it intended I should march

yet I find in my face
tell-tell lines

and in my restless pacing
patterned rhythms:

when did I join
who inveigled me

and what are these slogans
I'm determined to make

from bits and pieces
of discarded visions?

Who is this skirt
strutting past the
blur of numbers

hands
twirling the air
and marking time?

OH YOU

Dark-eyed truth   you
one-dimensional lover
wearing your dancing slippers on your ears
and dropping them at my feet
as if they were mine

I with my pigeon-toes
and oversized dreams

FOURTH CLASS MAIL

What does it take to denounce
everything but commitment to the
reality of that other place
on top of the mountain

"Country Property Spots
for Retirement"

that is not yet paid for
or even purchased
in fact only exists
in the printed ad just
clipped out from THE WEEKLY
SHOPPER—

Even though repelled by the
touch and smell of pulp
and cheap ink
even though far from re-
tirement here I sit
squinting at the print
already constructing
my weatherproofed hide-away
and hiking to the rim.

Am I as desperate at I seem
or is my imagination
working overtime
for some oath I've taken
that in my heightened state
now conceives

future dreams
of a Super-Cult to which
I've paid my dues
for copping out?

WISHING

In the sky this morning
a blimp is blurting out
dollar signs
and as they dissipate
Ruggles snoozing in the sun
catches them
shooting them out again
in long ZZzzzzs.

Fitfully they fly through
the cabbages buzzing into the raspberries
landing haphazard in the corn
vanishing in the squash and beans.

A fresh batch catches in the
skirts of the hollyhocks taunting the
black-eyed Susans cavorting
among the Four O'Clocks and Bachelors'
Buttons finally tumbling into the
empty laundry basket by Molly's just-hung
nightie and Rupert's socks.

The basement door is waiting
they slide down the ramp
landing on Rupert's workbench
tap-tap-tapping on the tops of
Molly's jam, the jars of
pickled watermelon, flitting in and out
of the snouts of Peggy's piggy bank
and Tommy's tommy gun. They barge into the
coal bin and bounce on the keys of
Grandpa's broken adding machine the
pile of textbooks, poems by
Robert Louis Stevenson.

Travel through the
vents to the Master Bedroom
where Molly is weeping
and Rupert sprawled out next to her
with his bottle is about to pass out.

There should be at least a message
sobs Molly. Something free or half-price
that we could shop for
or something to make Molly stop crying
moans Rupert, or me dry up.

The sun grows hotter
the afternoon drones on
Ruggles flicks his tail and rolls
Over, dreaming of bones and biscuits
and four leaf clovers

while the ad man
grinning and puffing on his
magic cigar circles lower . . .

MAHLER FIFTH

We see the world in a tree
skinned and shivering
washed out of the sky
in the sky's breakage
as singular as a soul
shipwrecked

And from this tree
the rivers flow
erecting their pain
in a thousand tributaries
each band cracking the soil
and sinking into
a well of nerves

Paper-thin walls
like a scream give way

The end drops
uprooted

The soul snaps back alone

Dry-eyed we walk through the rubble
searching for bones

peace   peace
the world falls like a snowflake
we go through it with our heads bared

GUITAR

the instrument is skin
which the finger plucks

until the sound becomes   a cry
running vertically

TERIZIN

a young girl is floating skyward
the smoke circling her head
in perfect curls

suddenly she
turns in the light

and as the light opens
she opens her arms

this life
out of the sea growing

these flowers
out of the wilderness

in a moment's whim
cut down
reduced as if they had never been

listen to the waves   lis-
ten as they break
as they
fall against the shore

they fall like prayers
they say nothing
lost   lost
in the spray

these spring bouquets

my hands cupped
I kneel on the stones
I kneel on the stones
the waves
pouring through my fingers
I kneel until I fall
the waves riding over me
little by lit-
tle   my finger-
s breaking them off

guilt collects
in little amber beads

the repetition of pain breeding pleasure

love collects
like tiny shards of death

at the bottom of a broken vessel

it is the pure shape
the stone prism
water
clarified by wood

the pure shape of meeting
the small separations and the change
the leaving behind and
falling apart

the pure shape of pain
a child's wonder
when first discovering the
dawn that makes division
permanent

YOU WERE

slim and perfect in your tight-fitting
pants
your alphabets and ice lined up
before you   blinking on and off
as you seated the children
and picked up your stick

you knew where to begin
because it was always back where
you were born

you weren't hungry then
and your body was round and plump
as an apple

the voices
covering you like a sheet
on a warm summer night

so you always wrote about the open windows
the smell of heat and trees
gasoline and rubber
flak-flak-flak of the tires in and out of the wall
endlessly chewing up the dust
and spitting it out
over the motorboat whine of the midnight cutters

instant slamming of doors
and laughing
muffled voices of strangers

it could have been last year
but the lake was miles away
and the passengers were tired
going home or out for ice cream

what did it matter
the sky was a puddle of sweat
the neighbors drank beer to forget

then it was always the dichotomy
what you wanted it to be
and what you were told it was not

until it became on its own
the cherry tree
or Santa Maria del Fiora
thick-lipped Mrs. Goldstein with the
mole on her chin

the stick wavers
the sun gives in
several centuries pass over you like clouds

and from your eyes the incubus
threatens you to begin Book Two

it was snowing that day
did you worry about the birds
coming back too soon
or tulips whose heads would be nipped

now the children sit up
they're instructed to listen
as if they'd never heard it before
never witnessed that knife that left
heart-shaped scars

voices that ran from them like blood

would they be disappointed
when all you can do is
open the door

no one can eat poetry you say
and the sunset is all in your head

Book Two is only a continuation of Book One
And Book Three is the same as Book Four
The hieroglyphic *flak-flak-flak* of the tires
Santa Maria and aging flab of the metaphor

you sit down   no applause
in fact not even silence
for the people are buzzing about
punctuation   and in the second-to-last poem
the way that man leaned against the pole
was he holding it up
or was it part of him
like an extra limb
what about syntax

it's 12 o'clock
the children are hungry
you smile   then suddenly you remember your own
hunger as you put down your stick
the words crumbling in your hands

SANCTUARY II

It was a strange captivity
too festive I thought

with flags and flowers everywhere
like some royal court

without courtiers   in fact
the people were quite plain and

if there was a king
he certainly wasn't Here

He the question Who!

and why was it "captivity"
I could have left
no one was forcing me to listen

the space between bars is
intentional   it

holds up other columns

"Lord Thou hast given me a cell/Wherein to dwell."
–Robert Herrick, *Hesperides*, "A Thanksgiving to God for His House"

we move from room to room
viewing these apparitions
but what we have paid to see
has been roped off

IN THE PHOTOGRAPH

a parrot is perched
on the shoulder of a naked woman

in her arms the infant cries
waging war in her face

THE KITE

Painting by Vo-Dinh of Vietnam

strolling into the sun
the pink-cheeked juene-fille
is carried along by the cloud
which she clasps tightly on a string
that is tied to her bonnet
while the not-so-little boy
(we do not see him)
laughingly jumps into the
sky after her

WE ARE THE ECHOES

we are the echoes
the refugees of echoes

gingerly we pick among the shards
pretending to search

searching for what
for we are fooling no one

there is no one to fool

even the ghetto is a hideous dream
and the nation so long
we have longed for
is finally a young heifer
growing into its own

yet where have we gone
and what is our promise

we who sit here praying not for prayers
but for miracles

we who call to the Unknown
only to mock It when it comes

or is the mockery only despair
the shawl we wrap around us
because we must

take away your echoes
we say
talking as if you were listening

find another place for them
another time
put them back in their boxes

bury them
or carry them so high
we will never hear them
even when they fall

they fall from us
still-born
they rise before us
standing on the mountains
like statues

standing on the mountains
and calling

MOTHER WITH CHILDREN

Ink sketch by Käthe Kollwitz

Oh sad eyes
Glad eyes
Little Pilgrim of Sleep
Awake in the night of knowing
Awake with the dawn
and sing until the sun that
sleeps in your limbs
lifts you up like a star

my face swimming in sun
I scrape
the long weed-green fingers from my lids

FROM A DRAWING BY KÄTHE KOLLWITZ

the chalk mothers are waiting
for their chalk children

but there's no comfort
in waiting

RETURN FROM THE SYNAGOGIUE

Painting by Marc Chagall

It is often winter
but the snow burns away from you
as you hurry home

and the icy tricklets licking your skin
slip through your collar unnoticed

someone wearing the same torn coat shivers
reminding you it is cold
but the word burns like wood
the fire spreading to your cheeks
that glow like two scarlet begonias

everyone should know what has happened
yet the others go on
like yesterday and the day before   still
huddled in their hands
picking nuts from the shells
or binding up loose ends with an
answer

they're tired
the week has been long
how could you even begin to
understand the weight of their
toil   bitterness of the night
with its burden of stars already
settling themselves like wolves
in the best chairs

she will be there to deny it
removing first the scrolls
placing flowers in the blue bowl
by the fire   plumping the pillows
readjusting the ladder

silent as snow
her heart overflowing
as she carefully unwraps
your weeping

PIETA in any language
is an invisible why
anguish of one who initiates
the open cry
imitates but never understands
the nature of that crude instrument
that carves heroes out of men

PIETA the sculptured likeness of love
what does she hold but her own helplessness
and where can she go but to her own
utterance

pity the mother's hold
the mother's hope
as unforgiving and dumb as death

PIETA

the same woman
sits before the gates
day in   day out

wearily plucking
at the emptiness

who is she
it doesn't matter

soon she'll be dead

don't weep for her
you'll upset the balance
she was young once
she had her dream

TO ERICA JONG

I heard you read last night
Erica

I knew your things before of course
I mean because why not
when they keep popping up
like pricks wrapped in my papers
or sandwiched between my books
like two tits and
blowing out of the anthologies
as soon as I open them

I find your lips on my mirror
They're often green
or smeared with sperm
like frosting
on a donut
dripping from the photographs of half-nude debutantes
or infant-mothers and their mothers-in-law
pawing through lettuce

I sneak a look at you
as I leaf through articles on diets and impotence

I mean because why not
when poetry until now
like an enameled egg
was guarded from grocery stores
just as it was guarded from
the mundane

now here is Erica Jong
leaping out of her cage
catching me in her teeth

and chewing on me until
I'm forced to listen

recipes for dissecting
onions
sixteen ways of caressing
a cunt   how to dye a pussy
pink or stripe it like a rainbow

stories of infinite orgasms
sign-language and interpretation in Technicolor
of each erotic scream
pictures of a dozen pricks on a plate
spoked out like a clock
from the strapped legs of their wearers

twelve cannolis rolled in cream
musical grunt grinning
from skins of primitive masks
syllabic no-sense
splattering white-gloved canvasses
tubes of poetry greasing
tanned bodies of tanned magazines

did you ever eat crabmeat from a cunt
or broccoli au gratin

so I hardly knew what to expect
as I waited for you
would you be as
beautiful as the girl on the poster

the one advertising shampoo
flying through the fields
with a lighted cigarette

would you bring your lovers

you were a half hour late
I was willing to wait
I would have waited even longer
than the moment
the room turned into a hospital
and a hush separated the audience
from the space in front where
a short large-stomached slightly
hunched mid-thirtyish woman in spectacles
almost as large as her face
adjusted the mic and began

at once I was reminded of one of my friends
in college who committed suicide
just before graduation
you even had the same grin
and your hair frizzed out around your
shoulders the way hers used to

behind those glasses are your eyes as blue as hers

I remember she was fond of performing one little trick
it's the sort of thing I think you would do Erica
so I'll tell you about it
she would place the tip of her index finger
directly in front of her eye and squinting
into it her other eye shut she would promptly
blot out the world   she did this often
like a child pleased with some new discovery
becomes obsessed with its repetition
performing it over and over
as if to make sure
the end will net the same result

but as you read on
I realized you were too old for suicide
just as you were   self-proclaimed
too settled for anything that exuded the odor of a cause

did you know your mouth twitched when
you spoke of Birdland Brides
and were you aware that every time you took a sip
of water you apologized for the Muse

oh Erica because I loved my friend
I love you too
and as I sat there listening
to your loneliness
as I sat there straightening your shoulders
straightening your hair
I suddenly wished you were pregnant
to hell with wrinkles
or standing before a kitchen sink
and crying over your onions

because I wanted to put my arms around you
I wanted to reassure you that cunts are ageless after all
and that cuff-links and tie clips
are only decorations for the husbands
you were so fond of boiling
and if you cook them long enough
and run cold water over them
before you crack them open
they will come out intact

who cares about the glasses   who cares about the size
of your tits

I still wanted to kiss you
I still wanted to kiss the poster

then I wanted to place
my finger in front of my eye
and as you stood before me
I wanted to blot you out
proving what

the inadequacy of your image

certainly not
you are full-blown

but more for the sake of my dead friend
I was committed to play
this little game

my friend was less than a year old when she
was brought from Germany by an aunt
both her parents ended up in Dachau
or Bergen-Belson, I forgot which
and her aunt had been blinded
how she got to this country without
eyes I never knew
it seemed a miracle that she was alive since she
too had been sentenced to death
anyway one day on the street in New York
someone held her up and stole the keys
to her apartment
when he broke in he discovered my
friend sixteen at the time
and he raped her   he
rammed a gun in her cunt
and with a knife he embroidered a large
chocolate soda on her arm

something else Erica   something else
that related more to the little enameled ovary
that I brought with me
press the button on the side of it
go on   press it   force it to open   let out
the little golden bird   can you hear
his lullaby Erica

I'm sleepless tonight

FIRST READING

AFTER WALLACE STEVENS

Sunday
leafing through the papers
and studying photographs of
flowering bougainvillea

while the snow outside
leaps against the wall

and the dancer down the street
choreographs obscenities
(only last week
another poet turned on the ignition
and today
the neighbors discovered to their
chagrin that the church had
blown away)

we couldn't help feeling somewhat
victimized
either by the elements
or the unnatural condition
provoking this unnaturalness
yet calling it natural,

while in Florida at that moment
the retired General was
squeezing oranges and
clearing the table
from his last campaign.

There were whole lists of shrubberies
we'd never heard of,
or if we had, here
sheathed in their Latinate

taking on an aura as plastic
as a plastic orange

orange related to cockatoo or mandarin
so did not exist,
the choice became ours.

Closing our eyes and jetting to Florida
where lying on the sands
we could justify what we laughed at (stripping
the names, stripping those ruins)—

because how could a church simply blow away,
and why for the poet
must inanition be sin
(while the ordinary meat-eating competitor
who greets each day with a grin)—

Yes.
It should be
the other way around,
a gamble at least
or a jest
for the one in-residence
radiant and free.

So we deliberated. Fig trees
From Teheran
or a miniature bonsoi shipped
direct from Japan;
the regularity of a hedge
or trees grown tall
that might structure something else
besides a wall
(poplars, the spires of a church
beech the back of a brow-beaten
philosopher)

enclosing what was both foolish and impractical,
meaning what?

That evening
as the snow crashed against the pane,
as the crystals built infinite cathedrals
and we listened to the *Second Brandenburg*
we added six forsythia
four pin oaks
and a scarlet weigela. Who could be blamed?

It was a kind of build-up of hysteria
low pressure at a high scream
wrote D. H. Lawrence
that could not be combated by anything
but art,
or sex.

It was still snowing when they came,
somewhere at the end of March
or was it already April—

dumped by the door
with the rest of the mail
and a package of socks
ordered the day before from a local
store.

A package no bigger than a broom
containing "forty-eight trees"
read the label.

According to the Almanac
this was supposed to be the mildest
winter in history
and in Florida, said the paper
the first alligator was getting

a heart transplant somewhere
in the Keys.

Tomorrow, I whispered.
Tomorrow we'll put on the *Mahler Fifth*
and dig forty-eight holes.
And as soon as we've listened
To the entire Symphony
we'll fuck 48 times.
Forty-eight
fucks under six dozen willows
six dozen pines
three thousand silver maples
and a flowering bougainvillea—

Proving to
the dancer and the poet
and even to that old Floridian general
that nothing and everything
is not un-
related to a certain Sunday desperation
causing us to order
what we didn't want.

FIRST READING

After Mark Strand

The introduction was short
summarizing six thousand years in the space of a minute
and summoning you
as if you'd been called upon
to fix the plunger in a broken toilet
or unlock the room past the one marked
COATS
where you now sat shivering (though
no one noticed).

Yet it was your name they called
so you strode to the front;
your hands glued to the book
that kept dropping
as your legs bounced from you
and a banana rolled from your lap;
somehow you began.

Carefully unwrapping each syllable
wiping your fingers
on your words, taking hot sips of yourself
pausing every once in awhile to look
up
as if half expecting the silent pilgrimage
to begin.

But when you got to the part about death
and God grabbed the book
when a monkey gobbled up the banana
and when the toilet really did let out a grand un-redeem-
able choke

suddenly everyone was running
for his coat;
but that room was locked.

And when they finally located
the keyman the coats
were dangling from the ceiling
like manikins
too high for anyone to reach—

So what could they do but go back—
noisily trooping
past the lectern
to their seats
where they listened
and forgot how cold you were,
and skinny, and how your words
never seemed to fit.

No longer expecting you to fix anything
while you ate yourself up
in front of them
consuming 6,000 years of history.

MALUS FLORIBUNDA

I've encountered you
in your arrogance;

perfectly postured
posed in the doorway
just coming in
or going out—

your spotless cravat
what mine is not
nor ever could be.

For you are King
of the Exedra,
your charmed circle surrounding you
and why not—
with your encyclopedic mind
and your name-dropping

with your exegetic air and your slight
French accent
or is it Greek—

how could you help but
captivate
everyone but me.

Is it the obstruction—the fact
that I can't get past—

or that familiar
throat-tickling . . .
How to begin?

So I start
with art.

Bach's Passions, Picasso's nudes
Stravinsky Lutoslawski Kandinsky Klee
Do you know Corinth and Klimpt—
What do you think of his famous KISS
Cezanne's apples Bernstein's *Mass* Have you
heard his Mahler Fifth whose Bartok
whose Beethoven
do you prefer? I ask I ask—
and suddenly
almost before it occurs—
I watch
as you turn
eyes leveling
head cocked
mechanical as a clock:

I blink—confused.
Have you removed your cravat?
Why
is it knotted around *my* neck?
And your coat—why do you drape it around
my shoulders?
Your mouth is
vanishing. In its place
is a snout. And your skin—
Why so pink and smooth?
Your wig drops to the floor
your eyes grow dim
and as their lashes
unfurl as your curlyque pops out—
My God, my Pig—Have I mis-
taken manimal
for manimus?
As it stiffens and calls

I'm lost Lover
Lost in your large
andante cantabile
shouting no
shouting no
shouting yes . . .

AFTER DYLAN THOMAS

The growing soon is cold
and seeping into every stop
is the trucked rubbish

promises and troublings
flapping like skin
always drifting back again
banked in blank beginnings

hear the smell of them
watch them grow
beyond the shadows
lost in gloom

as the large unsheltering
covered now
ungives the longing
frozen still

and the words come back
in stubbled scraps

while birds unchain
and the bread breaks loose;

chalk dancing in the bone
or puffed up in the spine
whistling and spinning

till the seed spills out
on piled-up tracks
and the steeples chime
lost upon lost . . .

the growing soon
begun.

HANDS: SISTINE CHAPEL

why are they so quick to undo
why so grasping
why unreal
touching
when they cannot feel
or feeling too much
so the feeling dies
just at the point of
meeting

you'd think they'd stop
clapping
when there's no one to hear

you'd think they'd stop
clasping
when no one is there

PROJECTIONS

projected on the wall are
hands curled in a fist and tied
with a handkerchief

we listen to the mouths of the
mothers and the mothers' mothers

and in the exhausted shadows between
watch the separation spawn
hideous rabbits

TERMINUS

This knot inside
is coming untied

it is growing
feet and eyes

and when I speak
it speaks too through

another part of me
deeper and slower

as if the voice
had just arrived.

When it can walk
on its own it says
it wants to go home

alone. It wants to be
free.

When? When?
it cries

expecting me to
give it the key

expecting me to somehow
provide

when all I can offer
is a paper pushcart

and an endless ride.

ADAGIO

I remember the laughter we ran through
the recognition
we were afraid to enter

and when we reached for it
reaching each other
instead

I remember wondering
what it was
at that moment
torn from us

that now
somehow
never occurred.

TRAUMA

what can you say
when your child
who faithfully recites
his prayers each night

rushes into the livingroom
with his broken
toy-death
and begs you to fix it?

PRAYER

I'm writing this
while holding on a long distance
call to a stranger
and the information I'm asking for
concerns a conversation between two
strangers
that has not yet occurred.

I've waited so long I know I should
hang up but if I do I will lose the
connection and all this time
I've waited will have been in vain

since I will probably have to transmit all of this
once more not to the stranger I'm waiting for
but to someone else
meaning the whole nature of the
conversation will have to be
altered in order to accommodate not two
but three strangers and not one
but two connections.

I am the stranger holding
and the writer writing
and I am calling you
I am
calling you
calling you
I am

I am

ALTERATIONS

when the doctor told me today
my eyes were getting
better for close-up
seeing
i marveled at nature's
compensation
that my distance vision is
so blurred i need glasses even
to recognize my own
decisions

but close-up for
reading or examining say
the anatomy of an
ant
as it makes its way
up
and down
the spine
of a leaf
wrinkles
lines
and other now more
noticeable im-
perfections
i'm fantastic

meaning that such rev-
elations let me believe
in myself
today
in spite of habitual
hang-ups
setbacks
lack of faith

and this
decision thing

and yet

today
tomorrow can always
produce a far-off
blurred percep-

tion of what i must
now see my way
through
eyes confounded
in order to accept
shortcomings of a closer
truth

that growth makes
deliberate detours
in order to
arrive by a
better route

BALANCING: THE FISHERFOLK OF FLORIDA

Even before dawn
on the coldest of mornings
one finds them lined up
on the bridge
with their buckets and bait kits.

Not young boys playing hookey
or workmen on a day off
but folks
who by wisdom or luck
have managed to outlive
their survival
and now have all the time in the world.

So for them
it's nothing stolen or snatched
from the ordinary
but more a resurrection.

Yet if there was a price for it
producing deficits of pain and loss
possibly this is not exaltation
but anger—revenge—

casting their nets
to catch anything they can
even with teeth that can't chew
and stomachs half gone.

Even when reasons have long
slipped away
they'll still
stand there staring at nothing
in particular
and wait
for the heaviness
or that impish pull
at the end of the line . . .

MATINS – COUP D'OEIL

This morning
I thought I saw
two deer frolicking in a far-off
field—strange for
them to be out in mid-
winter—were they
real or merely carved from
the air?

But then
as soon as I
spotted them
they stopped

their brown bodies
becoming field
white-dolloped tails
tufts of
snow—
quickly
decisively
in the next instant
leaping away . . .

Framed by the footlights
of the rising sun
moon-strobe slowly
yielding to a
band of light
melting down
the arctic night

and forcing out of the un-
expected
innocent shapes
that frolicked upon
the optic sphere
until awareness
in deer-like
recognition had
made them stop
and yet—

in the next instant
as if sensing
a “somethingness”
myself—
quickly
elusively leaping
away and

leaving behind
only a legerdemain
of remarkable
illusions . . .

MUSÉE DES BEAUX ARTS

About suffering they were never wrong.
The Old Masters: how they understood
The human position: how it takes place
While someone else is eating or opening a window or just
Walking dully along;
How, when the aged are reverently, passionately waiting
For the miraculous birth, there always must be
Children who did not specially want it to happen; skating
On a pond at the edge of the wood:

—W.H. Auden (1938)

Auden writes
the masters knew about suffering
and placed it center-canvas
perhaps to focus the viewers
on the peripheral sucking and chewing
of the onlookers:

the Breughel gang of Sears repair
persons Toyota dealers
K-mart counter help—you and I
and our unborn babies
anyone who has already survived his own
destiny or who will one day be forced
to transcend the aftermath
of still another Holocaust—:

Torture through the looking-glass
omniscient mini-views
featuring not the saintly
but ourselves
newscasts of helplessness
dissipated by commercials for
life insurance, prolonged sex. . .

For what appears as indifference
in the McDonald's parking lot
where rape or knifing
is coolly observed by a circle of
guzzlers and eaters
is actually a sacrament:
tribal praise-offering for the

juiciness of a Big Mac
in order to dismiss the perverse
pushiness of a god who still insists
the scales can never be tipped for
preservation without first paying
this damnable price.

Indifference in a crowd of Sunday
museum-goers who rarely pause long enough
before Rembrandt's portrait to consider
why he painted his real self
into the background
presenting upfront a faceless imitation or
"blind periphery"—
shroud for those Job-like
darknesses that hauntingly look out
and ask why, what for, what's the use . . .

Let us forgive and proceed
guiltless and celluloid:
our appetites indestructible
except perhaps by the announcement
of another Coming.

STILL LIFE

Let's talk about the things we keep
cartons of souvenirs
trinkets   bric-a-brac

pressed orchids and rank-smelling programs
dresses hats matching shoes
match-flaps sewing kits
salt-and-pepper shakers
Greetings from Canajaharie

hotel and airline shoeshine rags
paper laundry bags miniature bars of
soap unsent postcards

boxes of hand-crocheted handkerchiefs
monogrammed towels
tedious laborings of some long-
forgotten aunt
still starched and sterile in their
tissue coffins only one age slower to decompose than the
large
folders of newspaper clippings
recipes and records of trips
taken people visited lists of friends
for holiday card sending
correspondence
alphabetically dated.

Let's talk about the once precious
memories of taste and touch
objects of the scars
and recollections preserved
as if for another age
that would surely arrive
we must have thought
simply by the repetition of all
that was referred to then
as love

ORPHEUS

All my life
I tried to hear you sing.

I listened to birds crickets frogs
oceans brooks
fields trees:

Then one day you told me
to stop trying.

VENI VEDI

Item: Old Valentines in a
Shredded Wheat box

classic red heart glued to
a white paper lace doily with
I LOVE YOU in English Gothic.

Stylized Cupid
holding in front of him
a classic red heart glued onto
a white paper lace doily
an arrow through the heart

photograph of a nude woman
superimposed on Cupid
no arrow no heart

diagram of a human body
superimposed on a black-and-white
X-ray of someone's chest

coupon book for
heart-shaped pizzas
plastic heart-shaped
cookie mold

and finally at the bottom:
a picture postcard
of Niagara Falls—

powerhouse for shredding wheat
into a kneadable mash
stamped and pressed
into wheat-looking biscuits.

Perception isn't what it used to be
or maybe never was.

EXHIBITS

On the beach today
a vandalized "jon-boy"
euphemistic *nom de plume*
for any chemical non-flushing hole
that in pre-plumbing times
used to be a stationary edifice
often architecturally integral
to the rest of the house:

ivy-entwined
or decked with roses
and trellised vines
a far cry from today's
pre-fab thrones.

This one not totally decimated—
door still hanging
by a hinge
and only two walls gnawed-through
exposing its interior.

Not unlike the one on display
at the Art Museum
labeled SCULPTURE
carefully constructed
or vandalized from scratch and

not to be randomly encountered
on a beach walk
but deliberately viewed and
reacted to.
Even the orange stains
on the urinal
were authentic

seat crusted rusty paper roller
empty.

Perhaps this beach version was also
a SCULPTURE

Artists and Wreckers
occupying the same Sunday
pew, one called Crime
The other: "EPPA":

Existential Participatory Process Art . . .
creating "in the act of its Passion,"
states the Critic, "a *raison d'etre* that
recapitulates for the viewer the
same subliminal
craving to strip and expose one's
privates in a 'Pay Per View'."

Both were definitely statements
I thought, gazing out at the
white-capped roll
of waves heading shoreward.

OVERTAKING

Last week, the government (actually) approved the launching of the ashes of ten thousand into orbit . . . the Capsule of "cremains" will be boosted into place by a private company.

—Ellen Goodman

They're selling moonspace
not for ranch-types, Santa Fe's, colonials,
Wendy's, Burger Kings or McDonald's.
Not even for live entrepreneurs.

This venture is only for the urn gang.

Approved by the Department of Transportation
the federal boosters for free enterprise
in space . . .

God and His Celestial Airlines
will jet you there
so you can spend the rest of Eternity
orbiting your earthly self.

What a way to have your cheesecake and—
well—eat it too.

AMBER WAVES: AUTUMN WALK

In Boston they've erected a 35,000-piece miniature replica of the entire U.S. arsenal, and it is on display not as a work of art, even though from a distance, the off-white rose-and-light brown models of ceramic submarines, B-52 bombers, missiles and warheads that cover the floor and hang from the ceiling of the Science Museum's two-story lobby, have been created to look like a field of wheat. (Jan, 1986)

This morning
the fields are harvesting
shell-shocked children

dried sheaves of refugees
hostages

scarecrows nailed to
effigies of
dead heroes

drooping sunflowers clinging to
barbed-wire fences

Indian paintbrush crimson sumac
and bleeding flesh
add a finishing touch

and as I listen to the detonation
of my crackling feet
and push myself through the waves
of nausea . . .

somewhere in the back of my
head the drum-roll begins
and the life-sized arsenal of
impotent cries climbs
to a dizzying
crescendo:

*"Oh be-uuu-ti-ful
for spacious skies . . ."*

PILGRIM'S PROGRESS

Ordered well in advance
the freshest turkey stuffed
and trussed with rice
and chestnuts

and for this Annual Feast
the usual thanks
hands folded
heads bowed . . .

But wait—what's that
cloud boiling through the house
and that horrendous *smell*?

We race to the kitchen
just in time for the
inevitable BANG.

The world rocks
the sun stands still
we stand dumb in the doorway
wondering if we should call the
Fire Department or simply
let the innards burn off.

Should we laugh
or cry
for this is not funny
gobble-gobble—
it's ridiculous.

And yet—we remind ourselves—
we're still here; it's only poor
Tom who blew up.

Lovingly we garnish the blackened
heap with parsley, gherkins, radishes and
tomatoes.

BELIEVING

As much as we'd like to
we cannot anticipate the past
pretending tomorrow's injuries
are already X-rayed
for yesterday's pain—

Building a dream house on an invisible
lot and moving in anyway

Believing
if the key fits—
once inside
is a front door
to be opened.

What deliberate guile . . .
Yet we'd rather pay homage
to a sacrilegious clown
than an authentic saint
with a frozen smile . . .

IN A PLACE WHERE THERE ARE NO MEN

KENMORE DISPUTE BLOOMS

BUFFALO, NY . . . The daisies have bloomed again in Stephen Kenney's front yard and, once again, they've landed him in court. His tiny yard became a battleground last summer when officials of suburban Kenmore demanded that Kenney cut the growth of asters, cornflowers, gentians and other species. Kenney who planted many of the wildflowers, refused. An appeal of Kenney's conviction for violating the village building code will be heard today in Erie Court.

Today Stephen Kenney
a homeowner in Kenmore New York
is going to court.

For in Kenmore New York
daisies and dandelions are not only
frowned upon but
forbidden
learned Stephen
when he planted them as
surrogate lawn for grass.

Daisies and dandelions
do not belong on anyone's
front lawn ruled the residents
of Kenmore New York.
So Stephen Kenney is going to court.

Kenney is not a criminal or activist.
He's never deliberately disturbed
the peace.

He's an artist
who merely likes to fantasize about

fucking on flowered carpets
sprawled out nude
fondling astors and gentians--
loves me loves me not—

But the court ruled
and the residents
are adamant.

Of course he will appeal
for he is an artist
and no artist can survive
on conventional sex.

But poor Kenney seems doomed
to lose his case
unless he consents to a compromise:

Planting grass outside
and bringing his ass inside
with the daisies
where he can try to do his thing
on real carpet
before they wilt—

But he won't. What artist will settle
For second class?
He's no one's lackey, he harbors
no guilt and has too much to express
about fresh air, dirt, flies and feces . . .
No. He will *not* pay his dues
and must communicate with the Muse
his way.

So today in Kenmore New York
Stephen Kenney goes to court
for courting wildflowers.
And beauty's prosecutors
with propertied rights
on the grounds of truth
THEIR GROUNDS
will have him condemned
for publicly cultivating
self-abuse.

FOR PHILIP SCHULTZ WHO HAD AN UNCLE ABE ABOUT WHOM HE WROTE A POEM

Philip
I too had an Uncle Abe.

Hardly a prophet or patriarch
he certainly spoke no Scriptures
unless in those sacred books
I've overlooked passages about cheap
bourbon and discount deli's.

For me Abe's younger brother Moe
was more of a winner
(even though a cheek-and-arm pincher);
but I suffered the pain
because Uncle Moe was also the Candy Man:
large Hershey bars he'd fish out of his
pockets and slap into my hands.

When he laughed
which was often and at
nothing in particular
he tittered "*Tee-hee*"
in a titillating falsetto
which meant, said my mother
he had no balls.

Uncle Abe belonged to Aunt Mae who had
two sets of double chins and dyed her hair black
because she was Veronica Lake, but with
all that makeup I thought looked more like a
Russian coffee cake.

At night even her teeth lit up
her bosom was a bazaar of brooches and pins
her dozens of fingers a carnival of

rings. Winter and summer
all four feet of her wriggled and writhed with
dead minks whose heads
when she pressed a button
came alive: rolling their eyes
while their jaws snapped and to her delight
delivered a mean bite.

Uncle Moe was married to a fat mouse
named Tilly, but here God broke the
rules; Moe's voice had
the squeak and Tillie's was as low as
Mosie's was high. When someone
wound Tillie up she'd wiggle her whiskers
let out a sigh and deliver *molto sotto*[1]
from her bottom-most parts:
NUUUUUUUUU?"

All four were in the wholesale jewelry business
And even though already a generation removed
from gabardines and pushcart *shtetlry*[2]
even though they'd shaved off their forelocks
and given up *shul*[3]
a Christian was still a *shiksa*[4] or *goy*[5]
a Jew a Jew.

The last of the sextet was Aunt Isadore
and Uncle Rose
or was it the other way around
since Isadore wore the pants.

---

[1] much below one's normal voice range or pitch

[2] town characteristics (Yiddish)

[3] synagogue (Yiddish)

[4] a non-Jewish female (Yiddish)

[5] a non-Jewish person (Yiddish)

Rose was called Tootsie—"Tootsie Rose"
after the caramels I supposed—until I was
old enough to know better:
she always had large bowls visible.
The airless stairwell to their eighth story
flat was a trap for chicken soup smells
onions and schmaltz. Daughters
Mary Beth and Cindy Lou
predictably intermarried
and flew the coop.

The three Uncles sold diamonds all day
while the three Aunties played bridge
nibbled on bridge mix and boiled
chickens; and

Whatever friends they had apparently
did the same, since their talk
and smells were identical.

But—fellow poet—fellow Jew
why am I telling you all this?
What's the purpose of caricaturing the
Past, unless I'm guessing you too
as a fourth generation breakaway
in this cosmic condo that we're whirling around in
might also feel pulled at times
to reprogram yourself
to unfog the mirror and discover
a *landsman*[6]:

Do you also have Yom Kippur twinges
now that you've sold your lentils for a
running suit
forfeited farfel for trail mix

---

[6] someone from the same town (Yiddish)

tossed out the *chametz*[7]
(stale crumbs of someone else's Yiddish)
and replaced it with wax epithets and
cellophane-wrapped jokes?

Even if nostalgia isn't what it used to be
I have to confess
I still have moments when I
long for one of those pinches or
tweaks
another mink bite, *schmaltz*[8]
whiff—or one of those

half-melted
pocket-lint-tasting bars of
bargain chocolate . . .

---

[7] Chumetz - bread, grains and leavened products that are not consumed on the Jewish holiday of Passover, as well as all food items that are not specifically marked "kosher for Passover."

[8] Schmaltz - excessive sentimentality in art or music

PURGATION

Try to pretend you're not who you are
but Ms. America: not only
born with pulchritude and the right
proportions but a proclivity
for keeping them

even after five children three miscarriages
a hysterectomy and over two dozen years
of monogamous chauffeuring chef-ing schlepping
cleaning and catering to the Cub Scouts
of the imagination

infinite numbers of illicit
affairs that inevitably peak to frenzied orgies
of self-abuse in corroboration with a comfortable
collection of enviable excuses to cover up the fact
that you know you really are That Woman

nor could you ever be happy
merely being a department store manikin
kewpie doll angel movie queen saint
or anyone else's narcissistic perversion.

Who else will be there when you need her?
And can you predictably assume
with seasoned impunity *They*
will understand your tears and laughter—

so when you knock and
open the door
when you say yes without
thinking
consider how close you were to
almost missing this once-in-a-lifetime
opportunity . . .

QUADRUPLE SCOOP NUTS AND WHIPPED CREAM

In the mail today
a matchflap-like flip-up
that is I read
a sample from *Paris*
of a Perfume of Passionate Intensity.

In the photograph on the flap
Helena in silk and pearls
cups in her hand
the head of—back view—
a voluptuous mass of coalblack
curls:
her current *amour.*

Eyes glazed
lids at half-mast
already in a swoon . . .

I lift the flap
and remove the perfume
exposing a second photo
life-sized of one fluid ounce of
the magic *Metal: Paco Rabonne 87,*
Avenue de La Grande Armee 76782 Paris.

Slim and chic
the bottle is a miniature skyscraper
in front of which is a chunky
lower case 'r'
that could be a Henry Moore outside
or in the marble lobby that ushers us
in to crystal chandeliers and
cushiony chairs.

Later
after our jacuzzis and saunas
after he's pinned the orchid
on my Parisian gown

lights dimmed
champagne wheeled in
directly before the Musak begins:
an ominous hush.
And then . . .
a rush and a roar like
thousands of washing machines
all starting up—
out of the ducts pours—
How shall I describe
that delicious fragrance?

A cross between hyacinth and just-baked
chocolate chip cookies
apple blossoms
Johnson's Baby Powder
fabric softener and
hotdogs? . . .

My throat tightens
my teeth grow numb
and I feel myself lifting . . .
I begin to spin like a stand of
airport paperbacks
the lowercase 'r's riding the round
going up coming down
"*Paco Rabanne*," croons my lover.
"*Paco Rabanne, Paco Rabanne* . . ."

"This is a sample not to be sold,"
says the fine print on the back
with a special price
for this introductory offer:
one-half ounce
seventy-five dollars.

"However, it is also available,"
says the woman on the phone,
"for slightly less
in *eau de toilette*
and spray cologne . . ."

REUNION

No one's here now
the voices picked up long ago
and bundled off

even the goal posts are gone
and here in front where the flag was
only a rope.

Yet inside are the same chalk and
sour milk smells

same clocks
cricketing reluctantly
forward—
what—what—?—

And as I roam through the past
pretending to know

as I peer through all the
soaped-up memories
I wonder—

Did I pass or fail
or if marked on a curve
where did I stand—

What can I count on
that has finally been learned?

Is there someone to call
a public phone
or has that too
been cut off

my coins dropped in
coming back too soon?

OLD HOUSE

When I drive past
it looks at me
as if it needed arms
and a lap

as if I could still open
the door
to laundry smells
and tomatoey stews.

No lilacs anymore.
Even the forsythia is recycled,
the roses are tarmac.

Lined up in back where the apple tree
was and the raspberry patch

chrome bouquets
mark the graves of the missing.

No flags.
No epitaphs.

WHATEVER HAPPENED TO MILKMEN?

Everything's ready. Streets
rolled out stars dimmed, sun already
waiting in the wings. In a moment
the sign that says Morning
will drop from a string
and the world will know from the
cicada tape

and aerosol sprays of
wheat and clover
it's time to
proclaim:

Isn't it amazing
how all of this happens daily
like clockwork

the wires never
fail, connections never
break—

SEEING

In the painting
the straight green vertical is a tree.

Part of it clings to the
riverbank
its roots dangling mid-air
the riverbank is a mound of
pubic hair
attached to black-and-white
thighs.

Clouds and birds
sun and sky complete the scene—

but all this only exists
in the mind of the viewer
for in front of him is
a little black squiggle in the
corner that could be merely
the artist's signature
who when questioned
says interpretation is unequivocal

possibly related
to the angle at which the painting
is viewed or
what the viewer had for breakfast.

The title "An Anonymous Gift"
is posted on a green placard
below

and the painting hangs in the
maternity ward of the city
hospital.

OPEN HOUSE

After Theodore Roethke

my mailbox
has a purple tongue

my shutters say yes
to the cold

and no
to the sun

all glass is false
windows flesh

and every room
is a carbon copy

of an unanswered letter
with the wrong address

MY HOUSE

The fences are trim
shutters painted
even the grass is obedient
the dog never growls

Like a good dog
he just stands there all day
next to his house
a miniature of his master's.

And the trees:
If their leaves should fall
though no one has ever seen them
even turn color
they'd probably do a neat drop
into plastic bags.

But next door
the yard is fenceless
walk overgrown
no dog
leaves everywhere
trees bare
and the house itself
only a stone.

This is my house
and I live in it
next door.

LATER

In my dream I was lost again.
It was another emergency
but no one
would believe
I had to get there
because he was waiting.

By the time I found
the boulevard with the
marble equestrians
when I finally flung
open the door
and tore through the
atrium
the bride was gone.

It was then that I awoke
wondering where my veil was
and who had caught my
orchid bouquet.

LOCUS

So I finally found a suitable place
on the edge of the unpredictable
only a few blocks down from the last
complex that even guiltless
seemed promising.

What a relief after all these years
of renting what turned out to be large enough
but often furnished with nothing more
than the usual rituals of setting up each day
to preserve the next
built-ins
enough conveniences with
plug-ins for every
desire except one.

If I listen hard
enough I can almost
hear a
familiar sigh . . .

ACCEPTANCE

Suddenly you are
my little abortion
snuggling into my arms
the prince I ignored

prize pupil
whose apples I laughingly
gave back
or in front of you
tossed in the trash.

Bearing my name
you are a gold plaque
I've sold
for chewing gum

silver star now
tableware or
melted to cover
silver hair.

You are my brazen
bovine body
sour stomach
foul breath

mouth inside
that rules my tongue
with the wrong demands

and tortures me
with fantasies
of perfect worlds
and immortal death.

DEAF READING

In front of us stood one poet
and two persons
both mouthing the same words
each voice miming the other

a play on words
or play on play—
who could tell
which . . .

they could have been
senseless vibrations—

Like a clown clutching a
bouquet of balloons
struggling to stay
grounded

Each gesture framed
by lips of an imaginary
echo

HEURISTIC DEVICE

It's heartening
to hear safety experts
report that most beach drownings
can be prevented:

that when the time comes
for major trauma
and water is involved
if you're careful
and know what you're doing

you might not necessarily
go under
and never be heard from
again

but in fact could even survive
long enough to live through
other drownings—and

maybe even that curious
and usually unpredictable wind
known as "undertow":

water rushing back to sea
through a break in the sand bar
after it has already been washed
ashore; thus producing a backward
and forward retrograde
swish-swash that if you get
caught in might provide
perfect condition for
panic
since you cannot do anything
except let the water do *its* thing

either by taking you to where
it's been directed by God
or Nature or some other equally
qualified adjutant to go
or inviting you to. . . well . . .

But: relax say
the experts
and indeed this seems to be the
key to appropriate behavior
in most situations
involving death or any other
equally unfortunate disaster.

Do we not make our own fortunes
and call them fate?
Why panic and create ill-willed
newspaper write-ups
or space-consuming obituaries?
No one's waiting for us at the
end of the line. So take your
time, they say. Over-chilled wine
or burnt peas should be the
worst of it.

Breathe deeply, count to
ten and simply swim parallel;

in other words:
divert your intentions
and pretend you're not trapped
but merely out for a Sunday spin.

Make no attempt to get anywhere
or do anything that might prevent you
from being helpless.
You *could* change your vocabulary
and call "undertow" "tinkertoy"
or "playdough" or "chocolate mousse"
but certainly not "runout."

Soon
They Say you'll find yourselves
literally riding the waves as if
they were mere merry-go-round ponies.

Cleared of all
Danger and
emerging from the inertia
of your own inanition
as innocent and free
as if you'd only been sprawled
out on the sofa
watching TV.

NOTHING BUT NEWS

On TV tonight they're featuring
starved Africans.

In the Family Room Richard
mixes a double scotch
adjusts the movie-sized screen
and stretches out on the Eames.

In the Game Room Richie, Jr. swigs down a
coke glances at the cartoon of
belly-ballooned stick figures
and switches the channel.

Janet is out on a date
Charleen away at State
and Stephen won't be home until late.

Upstairs in the Master Bedroom
turbaned and toweled
Mary Ann inspects her nails and
sips a martini. She
frowns at the lineup of cute little
monkey babies clinging to the G-strings
of their organ-grinder daddies—
but wait. Those kinky-haired Natives
must be "She's"—not "He's." Surely
such obscenity should be censored . . .

She wonders if the *National Geographic*
subscription has finally run out
and whether they should renew at home
or the Office. Why are they so scrawny
except for their stomachs and why do
the women let themselves go? She wonders
if her breasts would sag too
if she were black and old.

What are they trying to prove
wonders Richard
draining his glass
and pouring another.
Why is there nothing but news
wonders Richie. He burps, picks up
a paddle and searches for the ball.

Mary Ann sighs
and closes her eyes
dozing through stocks sports
weather . . . commercials for laxatives dog
biscuits diet coke . . .

HERE TODAY

I was living near Cape Canaveral at the time of the Challenger accident. Devastated by the tragedy, I sat down and wrote this poem, submitting it to the Daytona Beach News. *As always, writing seemed to be the only gift I had to offer others who were also grieving. The editor wrote back immediately and said they never published poetry, but had decided to make an exception. The poem appeared in the newspaper the following day.*

Christa
like millions of Americans millions of schoolchildren
I watched your smile soar up into the sky
and only seconds later
freeze then shatter
into millions of particles instantaneously chewed-up
and sent shooting into
a different universe
than the one that had been planned for you
to explore.

I, too, watched what I never wanted to see
yet was forced to witness
as if I should have known before it happened
that it was destiny—meant to be—
that your smile had to die
for *this cause*—

But then I said to myself
through tears that were too tight to come out
through the tight wad of unforgiveness
that like that forked cloud on the front page of
every newspaper
kept jabbing at my heart—jabbing—jabbing
to let all the blood out—

this is a lesson. You are teaching
something.

For what's a smile—here today
gone tomorrow—
Isn't it better to have planted *it*
Instead of just another flag—in a garden
that needed some perennials
that would come up on their own each year
and not only bloom but spread?
Isn't it better for our children to know
even if they can't have everything
that Santa Claus—like the Messiah—
really does exist—here and now?
And for every American—that apple pie and motherhood
have now been planted with a woman's
determination to make even stunted history flourish
in the same plot as our steady crop of
"spacemarks"
that the teacher back on earth chalks up
on the board and points to as the next step forward:

Now in the time already passed
recalling for the class that dazzling
spill-out of a deliberately courageous
over-tumultuous American democratic but universal
God-given smile?

On the beach I pick up the fragments
and watch how the sun reflects on each grain.
Soon I shall have collected enough
pieces to be able to fill in the gaps
with my own so that I too can say yes Christa
it is indeed much better.

RELINQUISHING

Tomorrow is easy, but today is uncharted.
—John Ashbery

If there could be some way of charting
each moment in the act of passing
God would have to be asked to
resign. No one wants to be told
what he already knows
before it happens

and by someone hostile to the cause of
omniscience having already graduated with
honors from that course and discovered
what he'd learned once he was out in the
larger world, useless. So perhaps we're being
saved that task by God himself
who like a gentle and loving parent
relinquished his claim
yet behind our backs
hovers over us with his
experienced revelations

allowing us to comfortably travel into
tomorrow with our caravans
of hope and exact blueprints
for our castles in the sand.

ELEGY

So when it finally comes
what can we say?

This death
as awkward and oversized
as an infant's head

queasy and uncertain
as the morning sun
when it pauses on the horizon
as if it too wonders where to go next
which spaces will be open enough
when God knows it can't help
but enter—

yet unlike mere daylight
no innocent invasion
no eagerness
that widens to illuminate—

not this tumor.

For it is more the slow pour of salt
in a wound already smarting

a fistful of dust
flung in the eye
for a deliberate blinding
that never holds
and has no illusions.

So nothing
except maybe the recitation
of facts
about another yield
fears that have borne their
fruit and are now picked clean

fields that must finally be
bedded down
by the sower's plow
and those who gleaned.

HOW I WILL DIE

When the camera stops
a laugh will be trapped
in my eye my mouth
half-open
the best part of me lying
on my tongue untasted.

Or shoulders hunched
hands clutching the dirt
about to spring forward
in the only race
I knew I would win

Or joyfully
holding out my
arms
about to receive
what could finally be
given.

Or maybe just whirling
like a top
seen in that stopped instant
as nothing but
motion
turning

a frozen spot
between news and commercials
soundless and
storyless
the station's logo.

Carol Adler, MFA's first ghostwritten book listing her name as co-editor, *Why Am I Still Addicted? A Holistic Approach to Recovery*, was endorsed by Deepak Chopra, M.D., and published by McGraw-Hill. Other publications include three novels, five other books of poetry, and well over 200 poems in literary journals.

She has ghostwritten over 40 non-fiction and fiction works for a number of professionals in the education, health care and human potential industries.

Currently, Carol is President of Dandelion Books, LLC, www.dandelion-books.com of Mesa, Arizona, a full service publishing company; and President and CEO of Dandelion Enterprises, Inc., www.write-to-publish-for-profit.com, a full service writing and editing company.

Carol's business experience also includes co-ownership of a Palm Beach, FL public relations company and executive management positions in two U.S. rejuvenation and mind/body wellness corporations, for which she founded publishing divisions.

She has served as editor of several poetry and literary magazines, and her career also includes extensive teaching of college English poetry, fiction, non-fiction and business writing, and conducting of writing workshops in Florida and New York State prisons, libraries, elementary, junior and high schools, and senior citizen centers. She has a B. A. in philosophy and English from the U. of Michigan, and a Master of Fine Arts in Creative Writing from Vermont College/Norwich University.

www.ingramcontent.com/pod-product-compliance
Lightning Source LLC
LaVergne TN
LVHW090951080826
845145LV00003B/972

* 9 7 8 1 8 9 3 3 0 2 9 9 0 *